GW00787877

Divided Lines

A Poet's Stance

Creative Talents Unleashed

GENERAL INFORMATION

Divided Lines
A Poet's Stance
By
Creative Talents Unleashed

1st Edition: 2015

www.ctupublishinggroup.com

Publisher Information
1st Edition: Creative Talents Unleashed
CreativeTalentsUnleashed@aol.com

ISBN-13: 978-0-9961476-5-1 (Creative Talents Unleashed)
ISBN-10: 0996147659

$12.95

Dedication

With loving hearts the poets featured in "Divided Lines: A Poet's Stance" donated their poetry for this publishing to help establish a starving artist fund for writers that may not be able to financially afford the fees of becoming a published author. All proceeds from this publication are being donated to said fund.

Starving Artist

*F*oreword

In a world of ever increasing advances seemingly created to make our lives easier to manage, envisioned to bring us together, to draw us closer, we are still in many instances isolated and at odds and validly apart. Something is missing, there is a snag, a rip, a hole in the spiritual fabric that we all see; yet we continue to fail to address.

It has been said by self-proclaimed philosophers, theologians, scholars' and politicians that the abuse of words can be a danger, there are those that believe words are a leading factor in what ills our society. Of this we do not deny in full, there have been abuses, history is but a melody to that fact, yet it is also true that words have the innate capacity to bridge, to heal that which divides.

Opinions, views, religions, nations, people, even love divides. The focus of this book and the poets here in, is to give breath to a wide range of issues both small and controversial that lie beneath the surface. Things that we are often hesitant to discuss. In saying that, I will offer that the role of a poet is not to persuade or to add more rhetoric to the static we hear. A poet's responsibility is to shine the light of awareness, to create a platform for dialogue, for healing, to gather up the images in an attempt to understand what we see.

Demitri Tyler

Author, Creative Director - Creative Talents Unleashed

Preface

Creative Talents Unleashed choose the topic *Divided Lines* because we felt that so many things are currently happening in the world, and our eyes were being shown the reality through our media outlets for everyone to see. Racism is still relevant and happening, politics divide us by our beliefs, religion seperates us, and our own self esteem and life issues are tearing many of us apart.

We simply wrote the Foreword and left it up to the writer to interpruit in poetic form what they personally felt was something that divides. Pressed between these pages you will find poetry regarding Religion, Slavery, Racism, Depression, Personal Identity, Abuse, World Issues, Rights, Legalization, Relationships, and many other topics that strongly generate personal opinions.

Raja Williams

Author, Publisher, C.E.O. - Creative Talents Unleashed

Table of Contents

Table of Contents . . . continued

Table of Contents . . . continued

Table of Contents . . . continued

Table of Contents . . . continued

Epilogue

Divided Lines

A Poet's Stance

Creative Talents Unleashed

"Church On One Side (Part One)"

Church on one side
Hate on another
Unhitched, unhooked
Removed from each other
Church on one side, hate on another
Half breathes freely, half is smothered

One stands on holy ground, one stands in the street
Never in principle should both sides meet

Oh but if they do, may it
Never be discreetly
Ever may these titans clash and endeavor bitter-sweetly

Separate the sanctified from the stained
In doing so, love cannot be drained
Distinctive lines should be drawn, but if an
Evil twin is mothered…

…Love could then be spawned
From church on one side
And hate on another

Tony Haynes

"Hate On Another (Part Two)"

Hate on one side and church on another
A true test of our talents
The challenge is on and
Earth hangs in the balance

Our quest for both is naturally illusive
Neither can be mutually exclusive

And yet there are those who
Need to take it
One step further
They steal the easy way and make it harder
Hating on the earnest souls in a never
Ending search
Religiously for love inside a church

Tony Haynes

Slave

Sore little hands of blistered grime,
Red chapped cheeks slapped by rime,
Your bruised tired eyes betray sad soul,
No crumb, nor crust written in your bowl.

You´re still a babe, yet now so hard at work,
Beaten & chained if you dare sleep or shirk,
Cold & matted, no clothes, no food, no bed,
Just society´s canopy hanging over your head.

The Americas, Asia, Africa & all Europe too,
Progress, votes & elections haven't saved you,
Centuries gone, forgotten, have flown fast by,
Your unshed tears hidden within your little eye.

The sweat shops, quarries & deep dark mines,
It matters not; they are still all society´s crimes,
To ignore it, to permit it & allow it still to happen,
Yet, we don´t break the mold nor rip the pattern.

Tentative smile upon your tender & quivering lip,
Never tasted clean water, never even one little sip,
No arms to hold you close & to dry your little tears,
No blessed Angels to chase away your very real fears.

Twenty first century & we´re known as modern man,
Slavery ended we´ve been told, that´s the leaders plan,
Yet slaves we still use of the world's smallest little tots,
Turning our busy heads away, not caring one single jot.

Sue Lobo

The Meddling Hand of Man

The beast is culled & the tree is uprooted,
Hewn, shot, cut down & now sadly booted,
It does not belong & should never be here,
The poor innocents shake & tremble in fear.

Man emigrated, discovered, travelled & moved,
Overseas, through air, on foot & long ago hooved,
Digging, planting & killing in those faraway lands,
Meddling in all, with their sick minds & sad hands.

Removing, taking, sending, to & from all nations wide,
Tusk, plume, seed, egg, plant & from beasts, horn & hide,
Placing the poor saddened aliens in hostile foreign places,
Now, same unhappy creatures hinder man´s natural spaces.

Aliens now not wanted, propagating, breeding & spreading,
Their awful presence, leaving men shaking heads &
dreading,
Defenseless species, no fault of theirs in these cruel lands,
Due to yearning of man´s greed & the meddling of his
hands.

Sue Lobo

Onyx Blood

Born on the circle of the sun
my innocence was kissed
by a melanin mist
that came up from the ground
and blackened my skin.
My armor from the sun
Could not protect me from
my whiter brother
from another Mother-
Nature, who always favors the fittest
genetically speaking
we disrespect our own species
by favoring means over genes
and homes over chromosomes.
Selling our souls for fool's gold
all we've known is what we've been told.
Instead of reading a book
we get baited and hooked
on the ignorance,
which becomes our reality
TV Housewives and Hip Hop.
While our lives play out on cryptic screens
it's hard to see behind the scenes
The War on Drugs--police brutality
so what we've been
is what we shall be.
Our history
written with the ink of onyx blood
has spilled onto the pages of our present.
Killing, lynching, spraying, beating,
dogs on leashes biting and eating
the flesh off my Fathers . . .

The Blood Spangled Banner yet waves.
So, I dip my pen
into the blood of my kin
as it cries out from the ground
with Abel's sound
Somewhere between "I Have a Dream" and "By Any
Means"
I hear the voices and screams
of Malcom X and Dr. King
shattering the corridors of time
like bricks through stained-glass windows
as blood, black and thick
gushes into my innocence.

Brian L. Evans

My Bell, It Has Tolled

Winter's sharp teeth
chomp down to my bones.
Unthawed out thoughts
freeze in my brain.
Even the wind now
so cold that it moans
as it slams into
my face like a train.

Silent scream-cicles
stuck to my tongue,
frozen tears adhere
to my cheeks.
Lost elasticity
of limb and of lung
and a backbone
so stiff that it creaks.

The missions filled up,
the shelters are too,
so I shiver and
shake at the station.
On rooftops, warm smoke
spills up from the flue,
some Yule logs
in final cremation.

Bundled up tightly
in scarf and in hat,
but in shoes no
match for this weather.

My toes engaged
in a tit-for-a-tat
against the cold
constricting leather.

My belly's been empty
for what seems like weeks.
My cardboard sign has
turned up missing.
The wind drowns out
my stomach's shrill shrieks.
Digestion my bowels
reminiscing.

Churches no longer
hand out frcc hot mcals
to people in
my situation,
since City Officials
put an end to such deals
in cities across
this great nation.

So this Christmas Day
standing here in the cold
invisible to
all other people,
I know for certain
my bell, it has tolled.
It rings loudly now
from the church steeple.

Corey Cowan

A Battle Against Depression

Shrouded by a veil
Of desperate desire;
Alas! The vicious hoards
Of barbarians soldier on
And defensive walls cannot
Hold back the onslaught

Torn apart by whispers
On a sickening tongue;
Trapped within a pit
Of fierce, jeering foes:
Nothing cuts deeper than
The wounds of callous lies

Injured by a nightmare
Without physical form;
Dirty, crushing memories
Paired with bitter disrespect.
Words of steel pierce through
This undiscovered hero's heart

Laura Clark

Privilege

Don't worry about me.
My kids will be treated fairly by their teachers at their well-
funded schools.
The talk I will give them will have more to do with
remembering to brush their teeth,
do their homework and clean their rooms than about how to
act with the police.
Don't worry about me.
When I wear my hooded sweatshirt down the street people
will know I'm cold or going to the gym.
I can take a shortcut through someone's yard and not be
questioned.
Convenience store clerks will not be afraid when I enter
their stores even if it's late at night.
Don't worry about me.
When I'm riding in the elevator of a nice hotel,
I won't be mistaken for the maid, the janitor, or a kitchen
worker.
I won't be asked to carry someone's luggage to their room.
Don't worry about me.
I can let my kids play on a playground and the worst that
may happen is a scraped knee or broken arm from falling
off the swings.
And my doctor will accept my insurance that my work
provides and attend to my child's needs.
Don't worry about me.
I will be hired if I have the qualifications and interview
well.
I will be given a mortgage for a home or a loan to buy a car
with only routine paperwork.
Don't worry about me.
I can go 60 or more in a 55mph zone and not be stopped.

But if I am stopped, I will not have my body slammed
against my car, face pressed against my windshield or my
hands cuffed behind my back.
I will not be arrested. I may get a ticket but more likely a
warning.
And if at any time, I call the police to my house, they will
help me, respect me and keep me safe.

Don't worry about me.
But do worry.
Worry because my experiences are not yet universal.
Worry because my privileges are still based on the color of
my skin.
Worry and act and make change happen.
Make equality a reality
Then you won't need to worry about me or anyone else.

Joanne Dingus

KC

His profile picture shows him standing on the beach in
running shorts,
The ocean breeze blowing against his bare chest.
He stands alone face toward the horizon,
Broad shoulders,
Slim waist,
Toned thighs wrapped in Lycra running shorts.
His first time bare-chested since her childhood, splashing
naked in her kiddie pool.
He had her breasts removed,
Because she no longer existed in him.
And for the man he had become
Her breasts were constant reminders of the lie that lived
there.
I am happy for him and yet I'm mournful,
I struggle, seeing the two red lines left behind, silent scars
I know will fade in time.
I try to read between those lines to comprehend his story,
Because my story is so different, able to enjoy being a
woman through all stages, and twice a nursing mother.
I can't help think of the women who are desperate not to
make that choice.
Women with breast cancer who choose surgery to survive.
But maybe his survival depended on this choice as well.
I click on his photo once more.
In it I see a new life, stronger now, a man at peace with
himself.

Joanne Dingus

Taking Liberties

A boy cried to himself while being raped,
by a man that was to be a mentor,
memories of a joyful youth being stripped away,
replaced by dark horrors of touch,
witnesses turn their back and ignore,
fear for what may be uncovered,
instead of exposing and protecting the truth,
turning in the taker of children,
all guarded their reputations,
silence of what was right and just,
instead they all took turns contributing,
to the helpless' shaking nightmares.

Masses pull together to be in one voice,
peacefully singing in an unified chorus,
speeches falling on deaf ears,
surrounded by violent guards of aggression,
armoured rage ready to assault peace,
intimidated until the attack on the defenseless,
pounding away on the ribs of those that care to trust,
even when the inflicted bruising is uncalled,
marching orders of the elected authority above,
to break the spirit of the people who put them there.

A little girl is rescued from a violent chamber,
of physical, mental torture,
that was inflicted by supposedly kind parents,
only to be put in a house built on more hate,
to be brought down more in a place screened to be a safe
haven,
by people that had a blind job to do,
that cannot see blood or hears screams,

behind a closed door they built.

People on a hill that are sworn to protect,
those that cannot protect themselves,
the masses that are told to trust,
beaten, bloodied, again and again,
by suits that have a mission to line their pockets,
just to listen to those givers like string puppets,
closed eyes , head turned from the angst,
of the spoken, common people who they are taking liberties
from.

Andrew Scott

Shhhhh!!!

I am there, among you
A part of you.
Cut me off
And throw me away
But still, I lie within you.
You throw me out,
Out of the society
And then come to me
In that abandoned place.
Actually, you do realize,
I am a part of you.
That mask of piety hides such evils.
Let's shrug this veil
And show your true self!
Let's call it loud,
That I am no different!
Let's hug each other and run away from it!
Don't throw me alone, into this abyss!
Don't, for God's sake, throw me
Into this hellish bliss!
For one day, you, your own part will be us.
Let's strip this hypocrisy from yourself.
Or help me out of this bottomlessness......

Fareeha Manzoor

Child Abuse

Screams banging
Children crying
Time takes a while to heal
A child's pain
Whom do they run to?
Who will speak up for them?
When they are hurting
Where to run
Where is their refuge?
Where is their safety?

There is a cry next door
I have heard it before
It is a shrill
It is loud then it faints
Should I or should I not
There is older men visiting that child
Who will tell?

That child has scars
There are secrets untold
They not bold enough to tell
That child has broken bones
Shall we report? On the other hand, keep silent!

I, a child once
NO NO NO!
I will not be fearful
Silence is not my defense
I fear no one
I fear no man
I am I radical

Divided Lines – A Poet's Stance

I am an advocate
Children everywhere who are raped,
Molested and beaten
There will be a time of confession
Time of tribulation
Poets causing a revolution
Writing the stories untold
Telling them bold
In addition, we say NO MORE.

Christena AV Williams

It Threatens Social Order

They fear me
What they fear is my strength
They fear my capabilities
I surprise them with audacity
In challenging them mentally
They fear confrontation
They fear creativity
They fear natural aura
They fear that I overcome hate with love,
Anger with kindness
They fear my boldness
They fear I can think on my own
What I represent frightens them
Black-bold-brave
I am a threat to the system of conformity
I am a threat to the world system
They blame me for riots- revolts-revolutions
They fear my conscious approach
They fear that I love myself that I am still\natural in –
Skin tones- hair- eyes- principles- values- standards
They fear that I am not a replica
I am firm in the choice of music
I am self-motivated
They paint me to the world as a rebel and terrorist
Is it true what they say?
That I- bomb countries and taking lives
Have I invaded?
Did I rape, murder, genocide, extinct
Have I disrupted lives?
Have I killed?
Was it I?
You know most of all what they fear

It is what they paint me to be is untrue
Therefore, they slaughter us
Turn others of our own kind against us
Why do they do this?
Because I am different
Difference is something they fear.

Christena AV Williams

Imperfection

I cannot be one of these plastic people
looking like aliens
to keep up in a superficial world
Never will I alter my reflection
with noxious skin or lethargic smiles
My wrinkles are crevices
where laughter and pain flowed
My sags have filtered
nutritious whispers and toxic screams
I want every imperfection
to tell stories of the hard life
I had to endure to get to where I am
I want to look in the mirror
and see me

Donna J. Sanders

Eternal Kinship

We parted our ways but never let the hatred bloom
You're my companion, my brother and will remain to be

Neither you nor I thought to presume
To speak our hearts out during the departure

Though you emerged into a nation, abandoning the bond
A feeling of contempt could not invade

The World called us rivals, induced wars
There was love for one another under the shade

When I came to you recollecting the forgotten days
I recognized your love for me never faded

Innocent clashes under the worldly maze
Could not indeed erase the bond we share

We are an epitome of eternal kinship
Divided by boundaries, we are united by hearts

We stand for each other in hardship
For we are brothers until we die

Shaziya Shaik

A Rose For Gaza

Gaza is a garden full of roses.
Stone roses.
Rock roses.
No petals to crush and bruise
to release their fragrance.
Only dust.
Dust and the stench
of death.
No green space left.
No sweet tranquility,
peace or quiet.
No escape.
No garden of Eden here.
No gateway to paradise.
Rubble and rock roses.

So I shall plant a rose for Gaza
in my green space,
in my tranquil garden.
I won't bruise it,
just gently sniff it's fragrance
and hope that one day
fragrant roses will bloom again
in the garden of Gaza.

What else can I do?

Lynn White

Bleeding Freedom

They tout freedom like it's not hypocrisy.
Freedom is illusion that most never see.
All freedom is limited by powers that be.
True freedom has yet to install properly.
True what is said, find freedom in me,
Freedom of mind is the only truth free.
To them true freedom is anarchy,
Yet they require their freedom to bleed.

Christopher Allen Breidinger

The Face of America

Broken families
Divorce settlements
Custody battles
Sixteen and pregnant
"Who's the father?"
She doesn't know
He disappears without a trace
Abortion?
Adoption..
Stillborn
Depression
Psychosis
Addiction
Abusive relationship
Another unwanted pregnancy
Rape
More felonies
"This baby will never replace my stillborn"
Abandoned children
Orphaned and homeless
Wards of the State
Parties
Boyfriends
Yet another pregnancy
She wants it
He doesn't
He'll pay child support
"When will I ever get married?"
"I don't want to do this alone."
He disappears
Without a trace
Naivety never wins
Devastated Grandparents

Ruined lives and futures
Unpaid child support
"The other woman"
DNA Tests
Inmate father
Welfare
Single Mother
Parole
More custody battles
She wanted better for her child
For herself
A unanimous climb to the top
Bordered
Decorated
With years of pain
Misery
Grief
Trauma
Unfulfilling career
Until crisis begets itself
Into a world unknown
To common man
Builds her empire
Sets her past to fire
In the face of an unforgettable Love,
For a presence
Advocating
For battered women
Another war exactly won
For our mothers and fathers
For our daughters and sons
For the compromise in between,

This is the Face of America

Sarah Herring

Ridiculous

You can fit in everywhere and belong nowhere
all that matters is that you're comfortable
with yourself everywhere
all the frustrations from society's constant dictation and
moral manipulation the need to keep up with someone else
says that there's something missing within yourself
yet some sit in discontent
when someone else shows enough confidence
not to always follow the nonsense
those that understand their mentality is part of their
individuality
demonstrate what followers love to hate
they understand that everything
the majority likes isn't so great
we all like some material things
and the temporary joy some of it brings
the problem is some get attached
to so many of the wrong things
looking for a status many times being reckless
just to make someone's infamous checklist.
There are times when I am rendered speechless
because some people are just ridiculous
when you stop trying to fit in
you stand out from within.

Veronica Thornton

Digital Wasteland

We might as well
have circuits and wires
entwined with our veins
plug a virtual simulator
within the chasms
of our useless brains
as the more we rely
on the mechanical
our social skills
become outdated
and two dimensional
doomed to evolve
by the advancement
of artificial hands
ensnared like rodents
within labyrinths
of a digital wasteland

Donna J. Sanders

Abortion

Whoa! Are we really gonna go there?
This topic is to taboo,
it's to personal,
to painful.

Let me just ask what we know to come.
Is abortion right or is it wrong?
Why must we chose?
Let's put it into a perspective not most consider.

A young woman, her life ahead.
A young male friend, no good intention to come.
An attack is thrust upon her by him.
Conception occurs.

A young woman, her life ahead.
A male family member, no good intention to come.
An attack is thrust upon her by him.
Conception occurs.

A young woman, her life ahead.
A male stranger, no good intention to come.
An attack is thrust upon her by him.
Conception occurs.

Is abortion ok now?
Is abortion ok ever?
Do we take into consideration the reason,

or do we just stick to the status quo?

Don't answer now,
for you need time to digest these words.
Instead, just think.
Think about what is said before what is done.

Alexis McFarlin

Life Pangs

We are starving
The food ran out yesterday
But it's not our day to get food
My siblings and I cry out,
Our stomachs grumble in pain,
Nothing but dry cereal,
to curve the appetite of the hunger pang

We start buggin . . . "What's to eat, we're hungry?"
Mama says "Come on, yall know what day we get food!
Food Stamps ain't till the 9th."
My head drops low
That's two more days
My siblings can't count,
they don't know how hungry we'll go

Month after month
The same ole story
Binge eating and hunger, our life, our glory
Cupboards rolling deep in food on the 9th
And bare as hell come the 1st
And straight up empty on the 6th or 7th

Deserts galore
When we come from the store
Steaks, shrimp, and chicken too
Our first meal on the night of the 9th
We live like kings and queens
With no limits too high

But later down the road
Our food is stretched thin
And dinners are gross

30

Hot dogs and chips,
Top Ramen too,
Nobody wanting to eat that day after day
But hunger,
Will force even bad food into our mouths
To fill the need, to stop the pain

One day I finally got nerve . . .

I asked my Mama why we ate like kings on the 9th
and the poor days later?
She shook her head and said "listen here
I feed ya right, and make your food
Don't question me, I'm not in the mood."

Still puzzled I couldn't help but chime,
But why the 9th
Why do we starve and wait for that date?
Less than pleased, that I dare speak
She snapped "my Mama did it, and her granny too
Don't worry, you'll get food stamps too!"

I grew up on the system
And vowed to leave
I broke the circle and learned to survive

Food Stamps . . .

I got to much pride
I can hold my own,
I don't need a free ride
I eat like a king every day of the week
I pay my way,
I need not receive!

Paige Turner

Self-Rejection

Although I really hate being single
The fear of rejection controls me
I get lost in the thoughts of what if . . .

What if he doesn't like me?
What if I am not pretty enough?
What if I am not his type?
What if I am not good enough?

I start feeling like I have to pretend to be what I am not.

Pretending to like his likes.
Pretending I look the way I look right now every day.
Pretending we have chemistry.
Pretending I deserve to be with him.

And so,
I cancel our date
There is no need to pretend.

Self-Rejection, keeps me single again.

Paige Turner

Divisive Forces

The world is divided
By divisive forces…

Governments
Create borders
And political maps

Religion
Divides on
Communal lines

Races
Use
Ethnicity

Money
Creates differences
On the basis of wealth

Power
Divides the weak
From the strong

Love demolishes
Dividing lines
And, builds unity

All we need
Is one religion
Called 'God'

All we need

Is one nation
Called 'The World'

All we need
Is one community
Called 'The Human Race'

If we throw out
Money and power
And all other divisive forces....
From the face
Of this earth,
We may get to taste
The real meaning of Unity,
Equality,
Harmony
And, prosperity

Vincent Van Ross

Separation

They shared the furniture between them
He took the chairs
She took the tables
He took the books
She took the pictures
He took the dryer
She took the washing machine
They separated the house
They shared the boards between each other
The bed was left
They could not cut the bed in half
Who would sleep on a bed with only two legs?
And none of them would lie in bed without the other
She made the bed
They left the bed
They drove their separate ways
They forgot the lamps.
He came back the day after
Took the lamp shades
But he left the light bulbs hanging

Mariane Kvist Doktor

Positive Reflections

Are you so quick to hate
based upon assumptions made?
Can you see beyond the surface...
to what lies within?
Why must you judge based on the color of my skin?

We are all more than what we appear to be.
More than any label or slur,
hurled in fear and misunderstanding.

Look in the mirror.
Study the image you see.
That person staring back...
is not only you, it's me.

Ana Leigh Sparks

The Other Half

Barefooted babes,
not a penny in their pocket,
huddle and shiver
with cold and fear.
Urban nomads
scamper like mice
through grimy streets.
Visitors pass through
to gawk and stare
at how the other half lives.
Take a picture
but leave this unholy place
before the sun sets
and the rats
climb out of the sewers.
A little orphan boy,
dirt smudged
on his concave face
asleep against a brick wall.
He embraces
his brother's frail body
with one eye open.
Fat Cats
in suits of navy blue
jingle with each hurried step,
stopping only
to pick up
pennies from gutters.
Their pockets overflowing.

Jo Resner

Take it Back

Take back
all the broken promises.
Take back
all the "I love you's"
Take back
all the pretend joy.
Take back
all the hurt you caused.
Take back
every misguided thing you are.
And please just
Leave me lying in the dark.

Ana Leigh Sparks

The Rage in Albion

The homeless man under the bridge had eyes that bled
And woke each night from his humble bed
He had no poetry or rhyme,
No joy, no consequence or crime.
He wanted only food and bed,
And spoke of Albion with fear and dread.

 He held a placard with words that read:-

**"ENGLAND IS A PLACE OF WOE AND DREAD,
A COUNTRY OF NO LAW OR GRACE
ENGLAND IS A DREADFUL PLACE."**

The Poet asked his name, and the homeless man said:-
"I am the Rage in Albion, I have no name
For I am England's burden, and I am England's shame,
Mark my visage
Mark my frown
I am the Rage in Albion
I rise when the sun goes down
And when the single mother weeps on the other side of
town
There will be Rage in Albion when the sun goes down".

The Homeless man under the bridge held a placard that
read:-

**"ENGLAND IS A PLACE OF WOE AND DREAD,
A COUNTRY OF NO LAW OR GRACE
ENGLAND IS A DREADFUL PLACE."**

Again, the Poet asked his name, and the homeless man
said:-

"I am the Rage in Albion, Poet do not weep
I lay wake at night whilst Albion is asleep,
My eyes once blue are now blood red,
I am the Rage in Albion, the living who are dead
And when the Poet weeps with sadness on the other side of
Town
There will be Rage in Albion when the sun goes down".

The Homeless man under the bridge held a placard that
read:-

**"ENGLAND IS A PLACE OF WOE AND DREAD,
A COUNTRY OF NO LAW OR GRACE
ENGLAND IS A DREADFUL PLACE."**

He looked me in the eye and said;
"Poet, do not weep,
I only rise when Albion is asleep
My burdens they are many but my heart is strong
And I roam in the night for the days are too long
Mark my visage
Mark my frown
I am the Rage in Albion
I rise when the sun goes down."
And when a little child goes hungry on the other side of
town
There will be Rage in Albion when the sun goes down."

The Homeless man under the bridge held a placard that
read:-

**"ENGLAND IS A PLACE OF WOE AND DREAD,
A COUNTRY OF NO LAW OR GRACE
ENGLAND IS A DREADFUL PLACE".**

Cecelia Grant-Peters

Cinematic Bloodbath

Violence in the movies
violence in the streets
Violence is everywhere
even in the sheets
of rain that fall and abuse you as you walk
Sunrays berate you as you walk and you talk
We talk about shootings like they're an abhorrence
When we eat, sleep, and drink violence in torrents
kids look up the modern psychopath in movies like they are
gods
Then we witness shootings
what are the odds?
The odds are pretty good as I can plainly see
violence is the main moneymaker on TV
Blame mental illness
blame the lone sod
but never blame the elites
money is our God
We work all day and then pay to see someone pretend to
die on camera
Maybe if you put your money elsewhere we'd see people
hammer a
few nails into the planks of sanity
Instead we pay people for their vanity
I could go on and on but I will not
Just remember you're the one paying to see somebody get
shot

Adam Brown

Bad Math

Our division adds up
To insufficient math.
You found a thousand reasons
To love me, and just one
Reason to leave.
I can't blame you,
You were talking to a wall
As I did not heed the warnings.
I was blind to the divide
Between you and I,
It was a windshield, only seen
With the rain falling.
You had a rock in your hand, cocked
And ready to throw, but I held
Your arm back,
Afraid to rebuild,
Afraid to fix myself,
Afraid to change.
A better man would have handed you
The wrench himself,
But I was a nut too seized up
In my ways to be brave.
Our division was subtraction,
And it figures...

I've never been great at math.

Ryan Vallee

Cannabis Daydreams

Living amongst closed minds
behind closed doors have a smoke,
Living amongst blurred lines, duck in the shadows,
for another toke,
Living amongst ties that bind, In a fucking skewed society,
Greed to fuel the need,
purpose not the number one propriety,
Power make a man sour, folks give up liberty quietly,
Shout the motherfucking facts!
Pass that bowl and give me a match!
I'll say what I mean, no sugar coating, total candor!
Ease my stage fright, by robustly filling the bongs
chamber!
Eradicate measles and small pox,
Cancer treatment a cash cow,
So people die, politicians suck, silver tongued fox,
Darkness of the abyss, depression plagues this poetic artist,
Elected one's lies, chemicals instead of nature,
shake my angry fist!
Would you die for me?
I'd die for you, if your cause be true,
New scientific finds, time for new beliefs and ideas from
different minds,
Let me smoke, dude, without worry,
you scared of how high I can climb?
Misinformation used for the youth's wrongful education,
From under our feet Roosevelt pulled the rug,
I call bullshit on what is said,
Mary Jane ain't no gateway drug,
Reefer Madness, a pile of lies,
a girl sick from chemo, still denied,
Tell the truth with your hundred dollar haircut and your

thousand dollar suit,
Why chemicals from a scientists still?
Why not an herb grown in a natural field?
Why not face the truth and the sanity,
not madness, reefer brings?
Make them come true, all of our cannabis daydreams.

Matthew deVilleaux

The 21st Century Decline

Since the dawn of time slavery
was enforced with a whip,
now it is quietly conducted
with a foreclosure slip,
a low wage &
sick days without pay.
A perpetual cycle of debt
to keep you confused,
disconnected and upset,
an obvious yet tragic sign
that we've begun our descent
into The 21st Century Decline

Michael T. Coe

Terms and Conditions

An insatiable lust for the dough
Quenching the blood's thirst to get it though
Masquerading as carefree bureaucrats in declaring war on drugs
Flooding the metropolitan area; sponsored by aspiring thugs
Striving to be the next kingpin
Wanting to hitch a ride with hope to escape the sin
Familiar vices surrounding various areas
Whitewalls confining the dangerous minds to breaking the barriers
That was set up to pose as the American dream
Bit players handed football numbers in this Ponzi scheme
So this concludes the tale of wasted youth; such a tragedy
Gatekeepers laughing it up in this cruel comedy

Lindsey F. Rhodes

50 Shades of Gray

All along the divided lines
Pacifists and elders hugging the sidelines
Those are preaching for justice and for change
Tensions arise for the relations have become estranged
Revolution being painted with an obscure brush
The powers that be infatuated with the blood rush
Blurred truths that goes against the grain
Complete control as the objective in order to maintain
Weak minded souls sculpted by Willie Lynch
A dark reality is drawn while the onlookers flinch
Searching for answers in this tragic mosaic
Same ole song that has become prosaic

Lindsey F. Rhodes

Worth

Currency in the current scene
A tracking of worth
Occupied by envy and greed
Distracting
The fracking of earth
Preaching equality
Teaching economy
Poverty's proving
To say that we're equal is absurd
Approaching the hottest of heat
Watching the planet just burn
Changing migration
The patterns of birds
No fixed destination
Go travel the world
Unravel, observe
Find your space
In this place
Don't be swayed by the herd
This comfort's deserved
It's not black
It's not white
Everything's blurred
Or buried or burned
Or covered in dirt
Now is the time
Like a plant from a seed
Come unearthed
Arise from the depths of the dark
Back to life and unnerved
That's the meaning of worth
Simply being yourself
And that feeling

Should never be work
Unafraid of the hurt
On display, on your shirt
Wear your heart on your sleeve
You've been meant to since birth

Riley James Neault

Book

Sometimes
Words are just letters
Strung together
Just shapes on paper
Sometimes
Words are just sounds
Spoken together
Just notes floating on air
Sometimes
Words are weapons
Just wielded by fools
Cutting anyone nearby
Sometimes
Words are life preservers
Just in time
To save someone's soul

Maggie Mae

Devil's Tattoo

Can't seem to stop this cursed I laid upon myself
Lay down on the floor screaming in agony

He won't quit banging on the door,
hard enough without all this noise
trying to find a vein I can still use

Can hear his sobs on the other side of the door,
my heart breaks for him
That is for about six seconds,
until nirvana takes me to utopia

Hate that my Demons are stronger than my will
How I kept this from him so long I'll never know

Feel like a picture on the wall where the sun hits it all day
Fading more and more every year
until nothing but shadows remain

My only friends left,
the ones that understand me are my Dealers
Only they know the need,
how that right hit is better than the best orgasm

You mourn the loss of the girl you fell in love with
all those years ago
Try so hard to be that girl for you,
but when I whisper I love you, I lie

It's heroin that I'm picturing in my mind, my true love
When I come down I don't know who I want more,
and that scares me

You pack but never leave,
the battered suitcase sits by the door
Hate watching me throw my life away,
but more afraid to walk out

Couldn't handle the guilt if I over dosed again
Memories of better times remind you how I used to be

I promised over and over to quit,
grabbing my arm, he said look
been marked by the Devil himself
can't you see the Devil's tattoo?

Yanking my arm back, I asked why you're even here?
All you ever do is ruin my good buzz,
go find someone else to fix

Marching to my room,
wasn't surprised he thought it wise to use the couch
Though I must admit I was surprised the next day to see his
suitcases gone there on the door was a note,

Babe,

I love you, but for my sanity I had to leave.
You need help, the kind I can't give you
So goodbye my love, you made your
choice long ago, its time I accepted it

Love you always,
Mark

P.S... His note was read at my funeral six weeks later.
I was dead and still my funeral sounded more like an
intervention

Darcy Brandel

Captured Demons

Her desires brought the demons to play
They bed her nightly, enjoying their stay
She gave them what they wanted to feel
All the while she could never heal

With every sunrise that she awakened again
Depleted energy was shifting within
Knowing that night would again soon fall
And all she would hear was the demons call and call

She wanted so badly to keep them at bay
No longer the desire to let them play
But once the door was opened and they were invited in
They claimed her their bitch and she couldn't win

Broken
Tired
Used
And abused

She couldn't take it, she had enough
Resorting to ceremony to drive them away
The dream catcher used to keep them at bay
No more demons will she ever lay

Raja Williams

Reassurance (Losing a Loved One)

Misty waters paint a picture
of cherished memories shared yesterday.
A somber mood falls upon us
as the wind of change blows our way.
A rare flower that blooms every season
has been picked by God above.
For His purpose and His reason
so that heaven can now experience its love.
Emotions try to test our courage
as tears stream down like water
against the ocean banks.
We are sad but not discouraged.
For In All Things We Must Give Thanks.

Damon E. Johnson

United We Stand

There she flies, in all her glory,
honoring the brave and fallen.
Colors, so vibrant, tell her story,
of 'One Nation Under God'.

Red, stands out, fearless courage,
integrity of men and women, sacrifice.
Devotion to the United States of America,
patriotic until their very last breath.

White, equality, fairness for all,
innocence from hatred, non-judgement.
A non-color, yet fiercely holding hands,
with the red and blue, unconditionally.

Blue, loyalty, allegiance to America,
perseverance against injustice.
Land of the free, faith in mankind,
color of Heaven, hope for humanity.

Life in America, often taken for granted,
the ability to speak without repercussions.
A country known for religious freedom,
determination, the sanctity of Home.

In the words of Abraham Lincoln,
"A government of the people,
by the people, for the people."
Our flag, represents ALL people.

A sacred emblem of our country,
she is a symbol of our birthright.

Our heritage, runs through our veins,
purchased with blood and sorrow.

She flies high, a silhouette, among
the blue sky, Old Glory, shall never die.
Desecrated, burned, stomped on, in anger,
her significance shall remain, for eternity.

Debra McLain

Imperfections

Freckled skin, eyes of blue,
curly blonde, sweet, times two.
Just an innocent, knew no shame,
life taught lessons, one cruel game.

Ugly, spotty, frizzy haired child,
words that stung, she still smiled.
Orphan Annie, clothes, made from rags,
sewn from scraps, her mama had.

Never fitting in, moving every year,
new schools brought, a thousand tears.
Boys were mean, they pulled her hair,
calling her names, it was not fair.

Bullies are mean, they have no clue,
what a lifetime of damage, words can do.
Years of taunts, killed self esteem,
she punished herself, to the extreme.

By fifteen, bones were found,
hips and collar, her soul drowned.
A pretty little girl, with springy curls,
damaged by hate, in a judging world.

Debra McLain

The Last Heartbeat

It was a day like any other day
an early Monday afternoon in May –
and she was already dancing with the Angels
as her mother read that farewell letter.

She fell limply from the white cliffs
to the ocean whose waves gently bathed her feet,
their susurration a farewell prayer,
then taking flight she rose,
soaring skyward -
riding the winds with wide spread wings
like a white seagull.

The last heartbeat whispered
"Forgive me, Mom
Now I'm happy ".

Bozena Helena Mazur-Nowak

Lines Drawn

There's an invisible line set between us.
Separating the various parts of us.
Parts that are tossed about
whenever a disagreement comes about.
What is this line really stating and projecting?
We both have our alliance and choose not to change
what status quo wants us to believe.
There is a line between us and in reality we are free to be.
Free to want and desire what is rightfully ours.
Why not give in to that freedom of expression?
We were intended to blend and just be.
Coexisting together in this life.

Stephanie Francis

Blue Sky Dreams

This world spins round and round
Angel babies on the ground
The pain brings us to our knees
How can there be this much hate
We need a miracle before it's too late

Bullets flying
People dying
The evening news is all the rage
Shattered pictures of days gone by
Lost souls left asking why

If we keep repeating the past
Our future will not last
Those words cut like a sharpened knife
Everyone has gone crazy or so it seems
We have lost hope for blue sky dreams

Jay Long

Fearless

I do not fear the world's kings
sitting haughty and mighty
on money piled as thrones.
They fear my teeth sharpened from
eating bread made from stones.
My ears have long become deaf
from the constant bellow of their praises.
Eyes blind by years of their abuse,
I shudder not at the hand that rises
to mercilessly beat me
swiftly into silent submission.
I feel not the sting of the whip
for my back has long been cushioned
by the burden of their sustenance.
I no longer cry, eyes having gone dry
from weeping constantly
for those who were forced to die.
I frolic in the face of fear
aware that kings are afraid of me.
They tremble as my shackles jingle
although they hold the key.

Charlene Elson-Gustard

A to B

To consume or be consumed?
To eat is to eat myself alive.

I'm starving from the outside.
My insides scream at the sight of a mirror…
Have I gotten thinner?

I shouldn't get my hopes up.
I see only flaws where life draws pictures on my skin.
They read: "You're dying."

I want to feel confident.
Not like this beehive bloated with a billion stings
that hides a queen I can't seem to find
because my bones imprison me.

I'm hungry… No, I'm fucking fat!
I'm a beached whale,
but beached whales drown when the tide comes in,
or die from dehydration,
or suffocate beneath the weight of their own bodies.

My hair has started falling out.
I've stopped menstruating.
I'd pass up my last meal just to avoid the frustration.
I had my first heart attack at twenty-three.
Maybe it was trying to tell me something,
but I couldn't hear it over the sound of the media industry
constantly glorifying the human body.

What's my favorite food?
A n x i e t y .
Because it's the only thing I seem to eat.

Divided Lines – A Poet's Stance

I can't focus on my income.
Too focused on my intake.
Calorie counting down my days:
Chips, salad, beef, cake.
A buffet filled with mistakes.
I regret the last thing I ate.

I do cardio at the gym, burning for hours,
but I'm just running from the ash
this phoenix has devoured.
My mind is a vulture circling the carrion
heaped atop a soul that my life has abandoned.

I can't win!
I know this skin God has given me
is not a dungeon I should feel punished in,
but a vehicle to take me from A to B:
Not Anorexia or Bulimia,
but anomaly to beauty.

Still, I can't see what others see.
The faces on the TV tell me I need to be a certain weight
I can't achieve; and magazines, and movie screens.
I'm binging on broken dreams,
only to regurgitate all the things... I can't be.

We're force-fed ideals that are impossible to swallow.
I tried to be what I thought was "sexy,"
but it only left me bereft and hollow.

An empty stomach is the same as an empty heart.

Food shouldn't't own you or define who you are.

You can't consume yourself,
because you'll starve.

Steven T. Licardi

My Neighbour

They say he is of a different religion
With a different God.
His festivals are different than mine.
He has other scriptures & tenets to follow...

But strange that this may seem,
I found him to be crying with the same colorless tears...
That also fills my eyes!
His blood was red like mine...
& somewhere inside, I presumed,
His heart was alike my heart.

He felt the same hunger when deprived of food.
He felt the similar pain when he faced an injury.

Then why...?
Why do we build these artificial boundaries
That say he is different from me...
Don't we have identical identities?

Only because he was born in the neighbour's house
That homes another God & religion,
Is he supposed to be my enemy?

Am I supposed to hate him
For some atrocity perpetrated by someone else
Who was also a part of his religion?

In fact, these genuine doubts hover over my head
While I look for the unity in diversity...!

Debasish Mishra

I Am

I am a Man.

Not just by genitalia or the way
I was woven in the womb of the woman
I thus call Mother
But, as well, by the ambition of my heart
That leaves me swung to and fro
The hands of failure and success
The battle scares of life, my heart knows well

I am Black.

Yes, it is the colour of my skin
And the rest of my African kin
And kin all over her blue and green face
It is my colour, but not the extent
Of my intelligence, ethics and morals
It does not restrict my abilities
And nor is it a cognitive dissonant
That I can be both black and highly capable

I am Gay.

A Homosexual.
Not cursed or blessed but just ruled
By the beat of the drum that,
Inside me, beats loudly
The beat of my heart
That magnetic attraction I get
When I meet someone
And happen to be taken by them,
Romantically, intimately and yes,

It just so happens that the person
Is the same sex as I

I am Human.

A Homo Sapien,
The same being as you
Breathing oxygen and exhaling carbon dioxide
Heart pumping blood through my veins
Just as yours fills your veins
It is my heart, mind and soul
That make me Human,
My gender, race and sexuality
Do not make me less Homo Sapien that you
I just am who I am.

Lawrence Mashiyane

The Workmen

Bullshit fermented on the soles of their shoes,
An iron curtain shaded their eyes from the sun's rays,
A start of a new day,
All to become the dreamy doll faces of the workmen.
The rain came and with it a flood of debt,
Their shoes still wet,
They walked the dried river bed that took them to town,
A dust of tax whipped their backs,
A cold wind condemned their skin,
But, in their lips and eyes lived eternity,
Slaves we remain,
But, let us not curse life.

Hannah Allen

Lost Tribes

A level of sacredness is forgotten and strange to us,
No time to greet the passerby,
Whose face you once invited to dinner,
To attend a feast of friends.
What happened to the lost tribes?
They are more lost than ever.
Sitting in front of glass screens,
Fermenting in the comfortable A/C,
Frost-bitten from dumb information,
Mad for technology, Sad for love,
Too concerned about famous names,
Obsessed with the false reality playing on a movie screen,
A blind masquerade of patient purgatory,
Hypnotized and phantom eyed.
Unable to see and speak to their neighbor,
A foreigner,
And I am mad,
I'd like to run far away from this estranged disfigured
place,
I long to return to my home in the hills that's no longer
there,
Where we danced to visions and dreams led by a heartbeat
sound,
I'd like to find my friends again amongst the forest stinge,
Naked and elemental.

Hannah Allen

68

Schadenfreude

Our words flourished
With reckless hate
With a raging tide
Of undue scorn

As we heartlessly
Skewered our wayward foes
And peeled away
The layers, of far-gone brothers

Fragile strangers
Were our treasured prey
The plentiful feast
Sprawled before, our hawkish eyes

For we've buried
Our frail sense of dismay
Beneath, the bloodied mounds
Of our pale

And long-forgotten triumphs

William L. Wright, Jr.

Attention

The flag of your nation...

Archaic fascination
For idolization
And declaration
Of superior designation.

A landmark inscription
To ownership depiction.
Brainwashed addiction
To ceremonial infliction.

I've yet to see a flag of any nation with a heart on it.
I've yet to see any flag speak of love and peace.
I've yet to see a flag that didn't have any blood on it.
Or wasn't used as a shroud for its own deceased.

Christopher Allen Breidinger

A Poem to the Forsaken

Remember my face, for I am a fighter.
Remember my smile, for I am a gladiator.
Seek my blood, but it tastes bitter.
Violate my hope, but still it grows stronger.
Ravish my innocence, and yet it will shine brighter.
Plead not thy guilt, for guilt inhabits conscience.
Ask not for mercy, for you stray from forgiveness.
Live for my ruin, I touch glory.
Eradicate my roots, yet history documents my story.
Swallow my pride, if deemed necessary.
Tantalize my thought, but it remains my sanctuary.
Invade my soul, wreck my walls,
pretend me an 'aberration'.
Nourish your antipathy,
here comes mankind's abomination.
Envy my free will, wallow in desolation.
Estranged! I am not.
Broken! Dream not.
Yielding! Rejoice not.
Remember the promise, for it fades not.
My Name is engraved on the walls of memory.
Hands of fate will sooth my agony.
Forget me not, my faithful enemy.

Houda Kefi

Black Like Me

Being a target of
Brazen insults and
Indignities... he walks
Around the racist mass
Of those who think of
Him to be something or
Someone they want to...
Destroy... in this Love for Hate
In the color of his skin...
You hate your race so bad
You choose to bring out demonic
Hues...so that this cruel disenfranchised
World could see all through history, torment
And pain... we've been beaten burnt
Hanged drowned and maimed...
He walks around pretending to
Believe he's part of this historical
Reign serving in the U.S. Air Force
He sustained loss of his sight for ten years
While living his audacious, still chilling historical
Work in eye witnessing race in humanity...
 Just trying to see...
What it feels like to be... in his own Words...
to be "BLACK LIKE ME"

Honoring Author Mr. John G. Griffin (1920-1980)

Shihi Venus

A Stand For Just Us

In a country where we pledge allegiance
To the flag of The United States Of America
To the Republic for which it stands One Nation
Under God, indivisible with Liberty and Justice
For All...Only the difference every day is ...Our
Justice falls...it failed our Schools, our children
Our jobs ...our Healthcare, our Finances
it walks around with hearts of serial killers such
As Manson, Hate groups, Zimmermans and likes of

Where can we go for Just Us...for our Safety?
If the system chooses to change whenever
it feels the need to become bullies in the eyes
Of our babies...yeah, we've seen it all before
Everything comes back in rotation...what is it
That we need to do...
We need to stand up get up stand up for our rights
As Mr. Bob Marley saw then, what we see now
Young children getting killed to satisfy the fearful
Hunger of the powerless ...they are and some of us
Getting stalked...Just Us...because they said so...

In the Constitution, Just Us will hold up,
The hard headed Just Us workers
While racism falls in place to protect their investors
Cry...but why, when we see the devil face to face
How do we get rid of Satan...by standing up to it?
And it's powerless... to the word of God...To Change
The Toxic Minds of Evil...So Stand up
Get up for your civil rights...No JUSTICE FOR US

73

There's no one taking ahold of your hand....
Never stop voting...know your
Constitutional rights...teach it to you families and
Mentorship each, teach so they can learn them
All state to state...because right now...
It's JUST US. No Martin, Malcolm, Luke or John.

No. NO JUSTICE. JUST US...DYING...

Shihi Venus

A Toxic Trance

I had a dream one species poisoned all the air
Filled it all with smoke
And they didn't even care.

But as Real as it may seem
It Was Just a Dream.

I had a dream one species poisoned all the land
Filled it with toxic chemicals
And I just couldn't understand.

But as Real as it may seem
It Was Just a Dream.

I had a dream one species poisoned all the water
Polluted it with chemicals
Nothin' left to drink, when the temperature was hotter.

But as Real as it may seem
It Was Just a Dream.

I had a dream that I woke up from this dream
And it was just a nightmare
Nothing was as it seemed

What kind of species would destroy their own water?
What kind of species would destroy their own air?
What kind of species would destroy their own land?

As if their own Extinction
Was their grand Master Plan

And then the sun came up

75

and I awoke with a Scream
I knew that it was True
Everything was as it seems
It wasn't just a Dream

Brian Crandall

The Phoenix

Pearls of wisdom, gleaned from tears
Born of blood and pain and fear.
Fire, consuming and liberating
A crucible endured in silence.
A Phoenix rises from her ashes
A butterfly edged in steel.
She stands and declares to her captor
I AM HERE!   I AM HERE!

Beaten but not broken
Bruised but not defeated
She is a survivor!
She emerges a woman
Her youth sacrificed on the altar of pain.
She spreads her wings and takes flight.

Unsure but determined
Shaken and weak.
Her soul is scarred
Her heart is tender.
She is tentative and untried.

Pearls of wisdom, gleaned from tears
The Phoenix screams to the sky,
I AM HERE! I AM HERE!
I...AM....HERE!!!!

Vallery Townsend

Through These Corridors

Where the Christ Himself scuffed up His knees
His shadow now pushed up against walls once deemed
impenetrable
Gliding gracefully through the ghost of change for change
with such ease
And free of pain
Where dreams have name tags pinned on fat back flies with
gluey white eyes
Nursing grievances and whiskey, projecting the lie through
a smile beguiled
Enclosed in silence
Where life sized crucifixes transfix empty, infantile,
reptilian mind-states
Symmetrically postured
Putrid & dank
Imposing some announcement artificially memorialized
Apposing only goodness
Profanity oozing from under every single door

And no one is passed over.

Through these corridors
There's a National crisis amongst the damned
A life hereafter is spoken on, but no one believes it, really
From the bottom up blinded to everything but want &
desire
For plundered pockets and dignity
Plastic cards & bank notes
Cut throat in turn coat and starched shirts
Fucking one-another
All impersonally conceived, mounted like false teeth,
green with the envy that Babylon- The "New Babylon"
has achieved

Into the nostrils death breathed the lie of life into an already
dead being
MACHINES.

Through these corridors
Mongrels and whores
Vagabonds and rapists
Saints for Satan control this monetary enslavement
Citizens are patients
VACANT.
Like a soft dick sliding out of a must & damp trap tricked
Docile little vermin again, waltzing with the mice, nibbling
at dangling bits and pieces of humiliation, slaver pouring
from off of lips
Life sized crucifixes transfixing empty, infantile, reptilian
mind-states
Where The Christ Himself once scuffed up his knees.
Through these corridors
Death speaks.

June Barefield

Even I'm Divided

Left hemisphere right hemisphere
My bodily controls pulled by dual strings
My father so stern and manly
Mother sweet and insipid
Father so bombastic yet weak
Mother nerves of steel
Nature has an underbelly
What is on the surface
Is the denial of
what lies beneath
Libido
Passive aggressive
Love
War and peace
Eros and Thanatos
Mars and Venus
Voices within my head
You're whistling in the wind
Dreamer
Be careful
What you wish for
Not because it could come true
But because you know not
What transpires
From simplest atomic fission
To mushroom cloud
From genetic engineering
To seeds of doubt
Monstrosities abound
Demons making love
To angels
Humans arise from such
Falls.

Language langorous displays
Lagoons and lacunae
The blank revelations greater
Than the black bustling ants
Crawling abysmally clamorous
Doing business
But doubts pool amidst certainties
Like stark white emptiness.

We read life
In between
The lines
Where divisions collide
Unity in ink
The ilk of
Graceful collusion.

Lend us the usurper's usury
The victims of acquiescence
Victorious
The imperialist inheritance
Bloodless acquisition.

The meiosis and mitosis of civilizations.

Amrita Valan

Silent Voices of Servitude

At the foothills of ancient Mount Li
lies a mausoleum for Emperor Qin
its beauty and scale
are beyond all compare.

While the legacy avows its apparent claim
the entire of then-China, he did tame
from common script to punitive laws
a vision was set for glorious cause.

Upon the backs of 700,000 men
was a Terra Cotta Army of 8,000 built
those without recourse, or gold to pay
with their labor, debtors were forced to stay.

A ruler's pursuit of afterlife majesty
would demand an army of parquetry
the land was stripped of gold and jade
flowing rivers of mercury were many made.

With his death, he took all wealth
into deepest depths, he buried all
his countrymen, he did not enrich
his glory, greedily, he fed.

Qin's army now stands in silent attest
a necropolis remains buried, at nation's behest
evidence for lives that were never lived
as shells of men, with nothing to give.

Baidha Fercoq

Vanishing Gardens

Vanishing gardens of West Bengal
your crop's delight are sipped by all
India's finest to offer, as tea perfume
savory tea with a lingering scent.

Withering corpses, stand to till your soil
as speculative owners, fatten their vaults
these owners have grafted from land and laborer
leaving shells of both, without any matter.

Indifferent government, turns a blind eye
workers now scurry, hoping not to die
perhaps to mine stones, amongst dry river beds
or maybe yet, into human traffic be led?

What can allow a heartless government
to rob a people of their pulse?
While business plunders all human worth
a desert grows of endless thirst.

Baidha Fercoq

Salvation's Helmet

Salvation's helmet protect my thoughts
remind me that I have been bought
I have been paid for
no longer have to be sins whore
no more
No longer my pimp
With its crooked grin
and a limp
No longer my John
Strolling along
Looking for a "good time"
No longer my crime
Get your hands off
Don't touch me
I said stop
Suicidal tendencies
No longer having the best of me
Touching my mind
In its private part's
Rape from the start
Of my thoughts and heart
My soul
No deep dark hole
I take back control
And give it away
It's a new day
I will not stray
I've been bought
Sins trap
Uncaught
No bite from the Fowler snag
You can keep your loot bag
Be gone from my sight

I fight
Day
And
Night
I take flight
On eagles wings
Soaring with angelic beings
HaHa to death's sting
In your face
Now I laugh
But I will not turn my back
Armored front
Double sharp sword
Not blunt
And yet I
I
Won't even move
Nor lift a finger
For it is He
Yes He
That stands for me
Without wait
Nor linger
Indeed set free
The truth in me
It is He.

Billy Charles Root

A Game

What is that string?
Which binds me with you,
After all those years of abstinence
Why can't we just cut it loose?

Was that something eternal?
Written before we even got this life,
A faded scar in our frail hands,
Or is it something we alone created?

Can it be our destiny?
To be together for a while,
Then separate to make our own ways,
Why do we have to live this way?

Or is it something vague?
With no clear meaning attached to it,
Perhaps nature's idea of a game,
Is death the only end to this pain?

Iram Fatima 'Ashi'

Invisible

I've wanted to tell you
for so long
but my words are lost
in yours…
You drown me out
so I escape
inside a shell
to hide—
eventually
losing the words
myself.

Sameen Carter

Misnomer

Not birthed in Dr. Frankenstein's monochrome lab
Sacrificed, but not on a bloody stone slab
Disrespected through language condescended
To a world of crass impulse dishonorably commended
If not buying kitsch with contrived care
They're just breathing wholesale the marketer's air
Only one reason for their continued existence
To part with a dollar at a fool's insistence
Immobilized before television's strobe eye
Battered by hailstorm commands to buy
If in spite sprouts a tumor of sovereign thought
Chronic commercial's chemotherapy now for naught
The goal is creation of spineless passivity
Passions yoked to oxen of singular proclivity
Brain furrows plowed, empty seed catchers
Prelude to invasion of body and mind snatchers
"Consumer" a title no better than slave
To tapeworms only it's all the rage

Bruce Newman

It's Just a Joke

Must have had victim tattooed on my forehead,
Easy target some of the things that you said,
Did you see me coming a mile away?
I'm still thinking about those scars today,
The more you react the more I win was what you said,
I didn't know what to think,
We are just joking we don't mean any harm,
Oh my god you are so serious, it's all about the charm,
A joke is where everybody is laughing too,
But in this case the only one's laughing were you,
You said you missed the abuse even though there was no
excuse,
Feeling the inferior, there was the hysteria,
Walking the playground on my own,
My knees begin to buckle when I was alone,
Sometimes it was a dream was it like it seems,
After the abuse, when you made me feel not much use,
When you're looking for any excuse,
After walking through the fire and the smoke,
To you it was just a joke.

Steve Lay

White Privilege

It's easy to ignore systemic racism and all of its woes
It's easy to ignore a rigged court system everybody knows
It's easy to ignore white on black violence because it's so
ingrained
Into our media, schools and is never really explained
I find it hard to see the truth through the smoke and the lies
when a white cop kills a black kid and then denies
having any murderous tendencies or KKK ties
I find it easy to ignore because of all the glass mirrors
the hopes and dreams of a people, and especially their fears
I have white privilege; that much is crystal clear
Another black man was killed while I wrote this
None of you even shed a tear

Adam Levon Brown

The Leader - an Arabian sonnet

We never found a way under his sway.
The elephant trampled us in the fray.
At Lion's carnal feast we did fall a prey.
The sun blinds us, but we still feel no ray.

For his sake, burning, we flared in his lie.
And his forceful flood left us high and dry.
His shady plot though stared us in our aye.
His sky made us vie to die, not to fly.

He was only bound by our own promise
To follow him and grow in common bliss!
His sweet song was but insane serpent's bliss!

Over our heads past and future gather.
In the desert we share manna, yonder,
Where angels and beasts will live together.

Brigitte Poirson

Silent Creeper

It comes from nowhere
Creeping in silently behind closed doors
Lurking in every shadow,
It knows no boundaries . . .

It waits for the moment you let your guard down
For the day you feel; not quite yourself
For the hour your energy is low,
For the second you have doubt

It's called . . . FEAR

And you just let it in
Let it take up space in your head
Let it alter your perception,
Let it change your mind . . .

Fear . . . It's a Silent Creeper!

Paige Turner

Dividing Line

Ego
Can drive a wedge
Between the best of friends

Ego
Can divide everything
From A to Z

Man from Man
Family from Family
And, Community from community

Ego can divide
State from state
And, country from country

Where there is ego
There can be nothing else
For, ego creates differences
And dividing lines...
It builds walls

Every effort
Towards building unity
Must therefore
Begin with demolition
Of this dividing line

Divided Lines – A Poet's Stance

Every effort
Towards peace and harmony
Must therefore
Begin by destroying
The inflated ego of man

Vincent Van Ross

Epilogue

CREATIVE TALENTS UNLEAHED

Author Demitri Tyler states "A poet's responsibility is to shine the light of awareness, to create a platform for dialogue, for healing, to gather up the images in an attempt to understand what we see."

We hope this poetry collection opened the door for dialogue, and created some thought provoking new ideas in attempting to understand each poet's stance.

We close this book with a poem titled "Bittersweet Melody" by Author Damon E. Johnson. We chose to end this collection with a positive message. Life is Bittersweet, and filled with ups and downs, and it is up to us how we chose to live our life.

Raja Williams

We look forward to interacting with you via our social media outlets when we share the poems from Divided Lines. We want to hear your views, and hope you will share them with us in an open dialogue forum. Thank you for your support.

Bittersweet Melody

You are the sound of laughter
and the first sign of spring
You are the yellow rose in the rose bush
and the cool breeze of summer
You are the steady strings on an old guitar
and the golden-brown leaf riding the wind of fall

I am the song of the weeping willow
and the cold rain of winter
I am the thorn on the stem of a rose
and the mist in the morning air
I am the dull beat of a new drum
and the wilted oak tree in the backyard

Occasionally, you are the dark cloud in the afternoon sky
and the ripple in the quiet stream waters
while I am the blue bird peeking through the window
Yet you are neither the squeak in the front porch swing
nor the picnic basket beneath an unexpected shower

I am the warm cup of coffee on the nightstand
and perhaps the sand between the toes of weary feet
but not the stone in the old lady's shoe
You are the rainbow after the storm
I am the kiss of the blistering sun on naked skin

You are the sound of laughter
I am the song of the weeping willow
Together, we are imperfect harmony

Damon E. Johnson

THE POET'S

Adam Levon Brown

Divided Lines Contributions:
Cinemark Bloodbath   41
White Privilege   90

http://adamlevonbrown.blogspot.com/

Alexis McFarlin

Divided Lines Contribution:
Abortion   28

Amrita Valan

Divided Lines Contribution:

Even I'm Divided   80

Ana Leigh Sparks

Divided Lines Contribution:

Positive Reflections   36
Take It Back   38

https://www.facebook.com/DrippingwithInk

Andrew Scott

Divided Lines Contribution:

Taking Liberties   13

http://www.andrewmscott.com/

Baidha Fercoq

Divided Lines Contributions:

Silent Voices of Servitude   82
Vanishing Gardens   83

Billy Charles Root

Divided Lines Contribution:

Salvation's Helmet   84

http://www.ctupublishinggroup.com/billy-charles-root.html

Bozena Helena Mazur-Nowak

Divided Lines Contribution:

The Last Heartbeat   58

http://www.blurb.com/b/5280269-blue-longing

Brian Crandall

Divided Lines Contributions:

A Toxic Trance   75

www.facebook.com/brian.crandall.7/notes

Brian L. Evans

Divided Lines Contribution:

Onyx Blood   5

www.wisdomsquill.wordpress.com

Brigitte Poirson

Divided Lines Contribution:

The Leader (an Arabian sonnet)   91

Bruce Newman

Divided Lines Contribution:

Misnomer   88

http://www.amazon.com/Bruce-Newman/e/B00WR2XZPQ

Cecelia Grant-Peters

Divided Lines Contribution:

The Rage in Albion   39

http://ceceliagrant-peters.com/

Charlene Elson-Gustard

Divided Lines Contribution:

Fearless   61

Christena AV Williams

Divided Lines Contributions:

Child Abuse   16
It Threatens Social Order   18

http://www.blurb.com/b/4148458-pearls-among-stones

Christopher Allen -Breidinger

Divided Lines Contributions:

Bleeding Freedom   23
Attention   70

http://www.ctupublishinggroup.com/christopher-allen-breidinger.html

Corey Cowan

Divided Lines Contributions:

My Bell, It Has Tolled   7

Damon E. Johnson

Divided Lines Contributions:

The Reassurance (Losing a Loved One)   54
Bittersweet Melody   97

http://www.ctupublishinggroup.com/damon-e.-johnson-.html

Darcy Brandel

Divided Lines Contributions:

Devil's Tattoo   51

Debasish Mishra

Divided Lines Contributions:

My Neighbour   64

Debra McLain

Divided Lines Contributions:

United We Stand	55
Imperfections	57

http://www.ctupublishinggroup.com/debra-mclain.html

Demitri Tyler

Divided Lines Contribution:

Foreword	vii

http://www.ctupublishinggroup.com/demitri-tyler.html

Donna J. Sanders

Divided Lines Contribution:

Imperfection	20
Digital Wasteland	27

http://www.ctupublishinggroup.com/donna-j.-sanders.html

Fareeha Manzoor

Divided Lines Contributions:

Shhhhh!!!	15

Hannah Allen

Divided Lines Contributions:

Houda Kefi

Divided Lines Contribution:

Iram Fatima 'Ashi'

Divided Lines Contribution:

http://www.booksie.com/ashi17

Jay Long

Divided Lines Contribution:

http://facebook.com/writerjaylong

Jo Resner

Divided Lines Contribution:

The Other Half 37

Joanne Dingus

Divided Lines Contribution:

Privilege 10
KC 12

June Barefield

Divided Lines Contribution:

Through These Corridors 78

Laura Clark

Divided Lines Contribution:

A Battle Against Depression 9

https://inspiredstoriesandpoems.wordpress.com/

Lawrence Mashiyane

Divided Lines Contribution:

I Am   65

www.lawrence2writes.wordpress.com

Lindsey F. Rhodes

Divided Lines Contributions:

Terms and Conditions   46
50 Shades of Gray   47

http://www.ctupublishinggroup.com/lindsey-f.-rhodes.html

Lynn White

Divided Lines Contribution:

A Rose for Gaza   22

Maggie Mae

Divided Lines Contributions:

Book   50

www.facebook.com/MaggieLogiconMaggieTime

Mariane Kvist Doktor

Divided Lines Contributions:

Separation   35

http://servantwriter.k-doktor.dk/

Matthew deVilleaux

Divided Lines Contributions:

Cannabis Daydreams   43

https://www.facebook.com/pages/MC-Devillieaux/1525696511044859

Michael T. Coe

Divided Lines Contribution:

The 21st Century Decline   45

http://www.michaeltcoe.com/

Paige Turner

Divided Lines Contributions:

Life Pangs   30
Self-Rejection   32
Silent Creeper   92

https://paigeturnerthinkingoutloud.wordpress.com/

Raja Williams

Divided Lines Contributions:

www.Rajasinsight.com

Riley James Neault

Divided Lines Contribution:

https://www.facebook.com/pages/Scribbles-Daily/428272270675623

Ryan Vallee

Divided Lines Contributions:

Sameen Carter

Divided Lines Contribution:

www.facebook.com/people/Sameen-Carter/10000894031146

Divided Lines – A Poet's Stance

Sarah Herring

Divided Lines Contribution:

Shaziya Shaik

Divided Lines Contribution:

Shihi Venus

Divided Lines Contributions:

Stephanie Francis

Divided Lines Contribution:

Steve Lay

Divided Lines Contributions:

Steven T. Licardi

Divided Lines Contribution:

A to B   62

http://www.thesvenbo.com/

Sue Lobo

Divided Lines Contributions:

Slave   3
The Meddling Hand of Man   4

http://www.ctupublishinggroup.com/sue-lobo.html

Tony Haynes

Divided Lines Contributions:

"Church On One Side (Part One)"   1
"Hate On Another (Part Two)"   2

http://www.douglaskavanaugh.com/

Vallery Townsend

Divided Lines Contributions:

The Phoenix   77

https://m.facebook.com/ibleedonpaper

Veronica Thornton

Divided Lines Contributions:

Ridiculous   26

https://www.facebook.com/philosophyinPoetry

Vincent Van Ross

Divided Lines Contributions:

Divisive Forces   33
Dividing Line   93

William L. Wright Jr.

Divided Lines Contributions:

Schadenfreude   69

CREATIVE TALENTS UNLEAHED

Anthologies

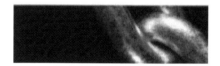

Preface . . .

This book is NOT for the literary critics or the interpreters who sit as gods judging what is and what is NOT poetry or who is and who is NOT a poet! This book is NOT for those in authority or those that prohibit authority of expression thus the title UNLEASHED. This book is filled with joy, lined with heart felt questions, marked with pain and will take you on a poetic journey. We will take the reader on a visionary quest demonstrating we "All" have the strength to preserver and see what we see! After all, people do see with different perspectives.

Yes there are sonnets to be found within these pages. Verses, stanzas, paragraphs and endings that rhyme. All the imagery and symbols that make up poetry can be found pressed upon the pages within, but what we, and the fellow authors of this book hope you will discover is. . . clear and accessible words with a language that speaks to you from the heart and maybe even alters the way you perceive the world.

Continued in Book . . .

100% of all proceeds generated from this book are being donated to the "Starving Artist Fund" that will assist writers in becoming published authors.

Purchase this book today! $10.00

Contributing Authors:

Jody 'Tru Story' Austin
Demitri Tyler
Shanese Whyte
Billy Charles Root
Elizabeth Esguerra Castillo
Kofi Asokwa-Nkansah
Shelley Fowler 'Ajee Da Poet'
Lindsey F. Rhodes
Raja Williams
Stacey 'Eloquently Speaking' Lunsford

Now Available:

http://www.ctupublishinggroup.com/starving-artist-fund.html

CREATIVE TALENTS UNLEAHED

Anthologies

28 poets from around the world came together to share and express in poetic form the emotion of love.

Now Available at:

http://www.ctupublishinggroup.com/starving-artist-fund.html

100% of all proceeds from any of our Anthology books are being donated to the "Starving Artist Fund" to assist writers in becoming published authors.

STARVING ARTIST FUND

Publishing Assistance

In 2013 after publishing her own book, Ms. Raja Williams quickly realized that there were many writer's throughout the world needing assistance in getting published. Her writing peers were reaching out to her asking for assistance and guidance in getting their own work published. Many of the writers were from other countries indicating that even accessing the World Wide Web was a challenge for them, never mind trying to find a publisher to assist them. Financial hardships were also preventing writers from sharing their beautiful poetry and words of wisdom.

Right away Raja felt inclined to assist her writing peers so she established the "Starving Artist Fund." A fund that will assist writers that are ready to submit their manuscript and become published authors at either a discounted rate or a full publishing scholarship. In 2014 Raja published our first book "Love, A Four Letter Word" with the help from 28 poets from around the world that donated their work to the publishing of said book to help establish the startup fund. All proceeds from the sales from "Love, A Four Letter Word" are being donated to the Starving Artist Fund.

When funding is made available to assist a writer in getting published, Raja will announce that she is accepting applications for publishing.

For More Information Please Visit Our Website At:

www.ctupublishinggroup.com/starving-artist-fund.html

Creative Talents Unleashed

Get Connected With Us!

Website: Creative Talents Unleashed Publishing Group

www.ctupublishinggroup.com

Facebook: Get connected with us on our Facebook Page

www.Facebook.com/Creativetalentsunleashed

Twitter: https://twitter.com/CTUPublishing

Blog: www.creativetalentunleashed.com

Pinterest: https://www.pinterest.com/creativetalents/

Instagram: https://instagram.com/ctupublishinggroup/

Tumbler: http://creativetalentsunleashed.tumblr.com/

Creative Talents Unleashed

Our Writing Groups:

The Writers Connection

https://www.facebook.com/groups/WritersConnection/

We opened up this group to have more flexibility in sharing. You are now able to advertise your book, share blogs, events, anything writing related is permitted to be shared here, with no rules and regulations. Take advantage of this group, and be sure to share your book and writing here as often as you want!

Creative Talents Unleashed "Writers Group"

https://www.facebook.com/groups/ctupublishing/

This group is for the serious writer, and does have rules and regulations. However, we are working hard at creating a group that supports one another and interacts with its members. Feel free to utilize this group, and interact with some fantastic writers.

Creative Talents Unleashed

Creative Talents Unleashed is a publishing group that offers an inspiring platform for both new and seasoned writers to tap into and participate with. We offer daily writing prompts and challenges to fuel the writer's mind, a variety of writing tips, and much more. We are honored to assist writers expand and grow in the journey of becoming published authors.

For More Information Contact:

www.ctupublishinggroup.com

Creativetalentsunleashed@aol.com

118

Printed in Great Britain
by Amazon